Wha
Moun

Shelby Braidich

The Rosen Publishing Group, Inc.
New York

A mountain is a group of rocks that has pushed through the ground and that rises high into the air.

The tallest mountain in the world is Mount Everest. Mount Everest is over five-and-a-half miles high!

Most mountains are near other mountains. A long row of mountains is called a **mountain range**.

Many kinds of animals live on mountains. A **mountain goat** can leap from one **cliff** to another very easily.

Some people like to climb mountains using ropes and hooks. These people are called **mountain climbers**.

It is colder at the top of a mountain than it is at the bottom. The tops of mountains are often covered with snow.

Trees and plants cannot grow on the tops of very tall mountains because it is too cold.

In the winter, people like to visit mountains that are covered with snow. It is fun to ski down a snowy mountain.

Some **tunnels** go from one side of a mountain to the other. People drive cars through tunnels.

Some cities are built in the mountains. Would you like to live in the mountains?

Glossary

cliff The steep, rocky side of a hill or mountain.

mountain climber Someone who likes to go up a mountain using ropes and hooks.

mountain goat A white animal with black horns that lives in the mountains.

mountain range A row of mountains.

tunnel A hole in a mountain through which people can drive.